CW01663104

EXPAT GUIDE: PHILIPPINES

The essential guide to becoming an expatriate in the Philippines

Disclaimer

General Information Only: The information provided in this book is for general informational purposes only. It should not be considered as professional advice on any subject matter.

No Professional Relationship: Reading this book does not create any professional relationship between the reader and the author or publisher.

Accuracy of Information: While every effort has been made to ensure that the information contained in this book is accurate and up to date, the author and publisher make no representations or warranties of any kind, express or implied, about the completeness, accuracy, reliability, suitability, or availability of the content.

Liability Limitation: In no event will the author or publisher be liable for any loss or damage including without limitation, indirect or consequential loss or damage, or any loss or damage whatsoever arising from loss of data or profits arising out of, or in connection with, the use of this book.

External Links: Any links to external websites provided within this book are provided for the reader's convenience only. The author and publisher have no control over the content of these sites and accept no responsibility for them or for any loss or damage that may arise from the reader's use of them.

Professional Advice: The information contained in this book is not intended to replace professional advice. If the reader requires professional advice in relation to any matter, he or she should consult an appropriately qualified professional.

Changes to Content: The author and publisher reserve the right to make changes to the content, layout, and other elements of this book without notice.

A word from the Author

"I found myself looking towards retirement with around 50% of my income. This is the standard pay for the pension system that I am proud to be a part of. In theory, a member could continue working and increase their pay percentage to 75% of what they were earning before retirement. However, this would require working for 39 or more years. My goal was to retire as soon as possible and start enjoying life. I realized that due to the lower income during retirement, my plans for retirement in America might not provide the level of enjoyment I desired due to the high cost of living. As a result, I began researching other countries with lower costs of living. Initially, I considered Thailand and loved my time there. However, I started gravitating towards the Philippines for three (four) reasons. First, English is widely spoken. Second, they drive on the right side of the road. Third, the tourist visa is easy to deal with extending to up to three years before you have to cross the border and return. The fourth and most important reason is that the people of the Philippines LOVE KARAOKE! I have a passion for singing, and it seems the people of the Philippines have that in common."

- *Jason*

Contents

Map of Philippines

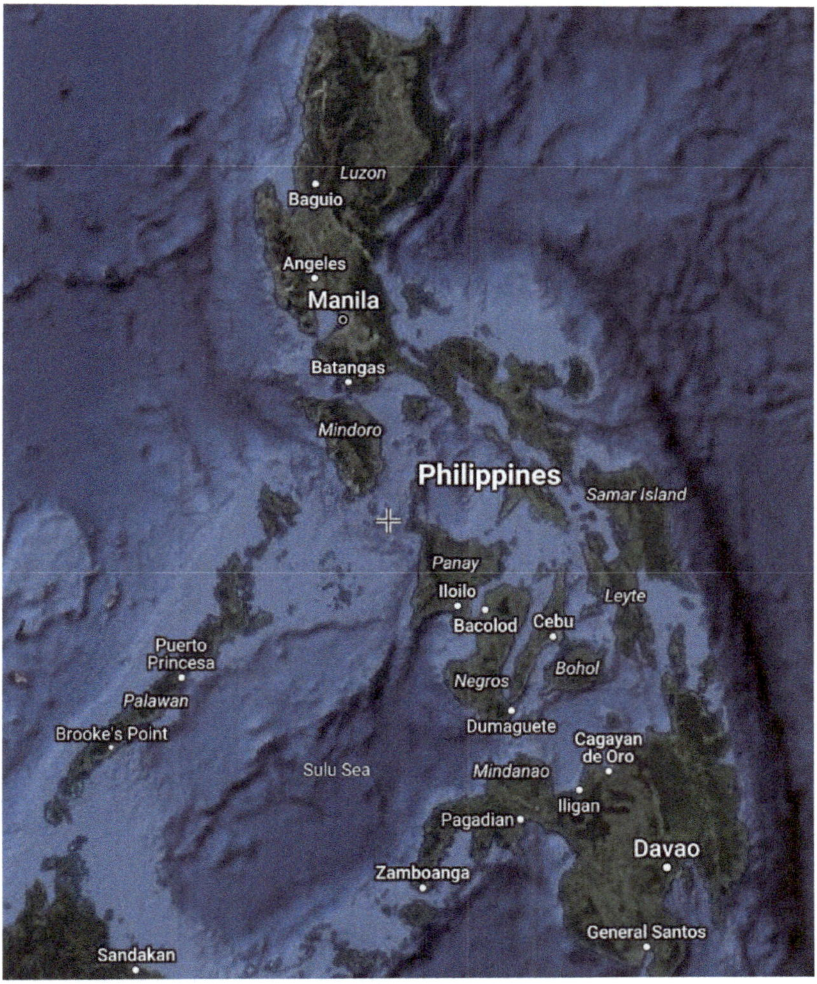

Understanding Expat Life

What is an expat?

An "expat" or "expatriate" is a term that refers to a person who has left their home country to live in another country. It is often used to describe professionals who have moved internationally for work, though it can also include people who retire abroad, students studying in foreign countries, or others who choose to live outside their home country for a variety of reasons.

Expats often live in their adopted countries for extended periods of time, and they may fully integrate into the local culture or choose to live in communities of other expats. Some expats maintain strong ties to their home country, while others may seek to become permanent residents or citizens of their new home. The experiences of expats can be highly diverse, depending on factors like their reasons for moving, the countries they are moving from and to, and their personal circumstances and attitudes.

Benefits and challenges of being an expat.

Benefits:

Cultural Experience: Living in a new country can provide a deep immersion into a new culture. You can learn about different traditions, cuisine, language, and ways of life.

Personal Growth: Living in a foreign country often fosters self-reliance, adaptability, and resilience. It can also broaden your perspective and make you more open-minded.

Career Opportunities: Sometimes, being an expat can lead to career opportunities that may not be available in your home country. Some people even get higher salaries and better benefits.

Adventure and Travel: Being based in a new location can make it easier to explore your host country and neighboring regions.

Learning a New Language: While this can also be a challenge, the opportunity to learn a new language can be seen as a benefit. It can enhance your skills and open new opportunities.

Challenges:

Language Barrier: If you do not speak the local language, this can be a significant challenge. Even simple tasks like grocery shopping or going to the bank can become difficult.

Cultural Differences: Cultural misunderstandings can cause social and professional difficulties. It is important to learn and respect the customs and etiquette of your host country.

Homesickness: Missing your family, friends, and familiar surroundings is a common challenge for many expats.

Finding Housing and Setting Up Utilities: The process of finding a place to live and getting utilities set up can be complex, especially if you are not familiar with how things work in your new country.

Legal/Visa Issues: Dealing with visas, permits, and other legal issues can be a major hassle. It is important to understand what is required and to keep your documents up to date.

Healthcare: Depending on the country, you might find the healthcare system is very different from what you are used to. It can be a challenge to find good doctors, understand the healthcare system, and deal with insurance.

Choosing the Philippines

Why the Philippines?

Warm and Welcoming Culture: Filipino people are known worldwide for their hospitality. They tend to be very friendly, welcoming, and helpful towards foreigners.

English Proficiency: English is one of the official languages in the Philippines, along with Filipino (Tagalog). Most Filipinos speak English, and it is also the medium of instruction in schools. This can make communication and integration much easier for English-speaking expats.

Natural Beauty: The Philippines is home to a variety of beautiful landscapes including beaches, mountains, and forests. With over 7,000 islands, there are plenty of opportunities for outdoor activities like swimming, surfing, hiking, and diving.

Low Cost of Living: Compared to many Western countries, the cost of living in the Philippines is quite low. This includes the cost of housing, food, transportation, and healthcare. It is possible for expats to enjoy a high standard of living at a fraction of the cost in their home country.

Strong Expat Communities: The Philippines has a thriving expat community, with many clubs, organizations, and events catering specifically to foreigners living in the country.

Business Opportunities: For those interested in business, the Philippines offers opportunities in sectors such as information technology, business process outsourcing, tourism, and agriculture among others.

Weather: The Philippines has a tropical climate, with a warm average temperature year-round. Some people may find this preferable to the cold winters found in many other countries.

Safety considerations

Natural Disasters: The Philippines is in the Pacific Ring of Fire, which makes it prone to earthquakes and volcanic eruptions. The country also experiences an average of 20 typhoons each year. Familiarize yourself with safety measures for these natural disasters.

Traffic Safety: Traffic in major cities like Manila and Cebu can be hectic, and road conditions can be poor in some areas. Be vigilant when crossing the street, and if you plan to drive, make sure you are comfortable with local traffic rules and conditions.

Health Risks: Depending on your location, dengue fever and other mosquito-borne diseases can be a risk. It is important to take appropriate precautions, such as using mosquito repellent and getting any recommended vaccinations.

Personal Safety: While many parts of the Philippines are safe, crime can be an issue in certain areas, particularly in larger cities and at night. Avoid displaying expensive belongings in public and be aware of common scams that target tourists and expats.

Political Stability: While the Philippines is generally politically stable, it is important to be aware of current events and avoid any political demonstrations or protests, as these can sometimes turn violent.

Travel Advisory: Check your home country's travel advisory for the Philippines for the most up-to-date safety information.

Local Laws and Customs: Respect local laws and customs to avoid unnecessary troubles. This can include laws regarding drug use, behavior in public, respect for the flag and national anthem, etc.

Political climate

The political climate in a country can greatly impact the overall safety, stability, and living conditions for both its citizens and expatriates living there. Here are a few reasons why the political climate is a crucial safety consideration:

Civil Unrest: In countries where the political climate is volatile, there could be protests, strikes, or demonstrations that sometimes turn violent. Even peaceful protests can cause disruptions to daily life, like public transportation shutdowns or road closures.

Policy Changes: Political climate can affect the laws and policies of a country. These could involve visa regulations, tax laws, or business regulations, which might directly impact expatriates.

Social Services: The government's political stance can influence the quality and availability of public services like healthcare, education, and infrastructure. This can impact the overall quality of life in a country.

Crime and Law Enforcement: Political instability can sometimes lead to increases in crime rates or corruption. In some cases, it could affect the trustworthiness and efficiency of law enforcement agencies.

Economic Stability: Political decisions can have a significant impact on a country's economy, affecting everything from the cost of living and inflation rate to employment opportunities.

As an expatriate planning to move to another country, it is important to understand the political climate, its potential changes, and its impact on your safety and well-being. Always keep abreast of the latest news and updates, and ensure you have plans in place to deal with possible political issues that may arise during your stay.

Socioeconomic factors

Socioeconomic factors play a key role in shaping the safety and overall quality of life in any given region. Here is why they are an important consideration:

Income Inequality: High levels of income inequality can result in higher crime rates, including theft, robbery, or more serious crimes. In areas with wide wealth gaps, expats—often perceived as wealthy—can be targeted.

Poverty: Higher levels of poverty can contribute to higher crime rates, poor health outcomes, and lower education levels in the community. This can impact your overall quality of life, as well as the range of services and resources available to you.

Education Level: In areas where education levels are lower, there might be less cultural understanding or acceptance of foreign residents. There may also be language barriers that make daily life more challenging.

Healthcare System: Countries with stronger socioeconomic status often have better healthcare systems and services. In places with lower socioeconomic conditions, healthcare services might be lacking or of poor quality, which can be a significant concern, especially during a health crisis.

Infrastructure: Socioeconomic status often influences the quality of infrastructure such as roads, public transportation, utilities, and internet connectivity. Living in an area with poor infrastructure can pose challenges to daily life and potentially safety issues.

Understanding these factors can help you better choose where to live within a country, how to prepare for the move, and what to expect in terms of local interaction, cost of living, and lifestyle adjustments. As with any move, research and preparation are key to ensuring a successful and comfortable transition.

Visa and Legal Requirements

Types of visas available

Tourist Visa (9A): This is for foreigners visiting for leisure or tourism purposes. The tourist visa is usually valid for 30 days but can be extended at the Bureau of Immigration.

Business Visa (9A): If you are traveling for business purposes, you may also use a 9A visa. The requirements are like those of the tourist visa, but additional documentation may be necessary, such as a letter from your company.

Employment Visa (9G): This is for foreigners who have been hired by a Philippine-based company. This visa is typically arranged by the employer.

Special Investor's Resident Visa (SIRV): This visa is for foreigners investing a significant amount of money in the Philippine economy.

Special Resident Retiree's Visa (SRRV): This visa is designed for foreign nationals who are retirees and wish to reside in the Philippines. It offers multiple entry privileges and is essentially a lifetime visa if the required conditions are maintained.

Student Visa (9F): This is for foreigners who intend to enroll in an educational institution in the Philippines.

Quota Immigrant Visa: This is issued to foreigners on a basis of reciprocity with their home country and is available to a limited number of applicants per year.

Keep in mind that the specific requirements for each visa type can vary, and regulations can change over time. Always check the most recent guidelines from the Philippines Bureau of Immigration or the nearest Philippine consulate or embassy.

As always, it is important to fully understand the terms and conditions of your visa, including the validity period, the conditions under which you can work or study, and the requirements for extending or changing your visa status. Non-compliance with visa regulations can result in serious penalties, including fines, imprisonment, and deportation.

Process of applying for a visa

The process of applying for a visa to the Philippines can vary depending on the type of visa you need and your country of residence. However, a general process often includes the following steps:

Determine the Type of Visa You Need: The first step is to figure out what type of visa you need based on your purpose of travel (e.g., tourism, employment, retirement, etc.).

Complete the Application Form: You will need to complete the appropriate application form. These forms can often be found on the website of the Philippine embassy or consulate in your country, or the Philippines Bureau of Immigration.

Prepare Required Documents: Depending on the type of visa, you will need to gather different documents. These might include your passport, proof of financial means, invitation letter, employment contract, etc. Ensure that your documents are complete to avoid delays in processing.

Pay the Visa Fee: The fee varies depending on the type of visa you are applying for. Payment methods can vary, so check with the embassy or consulate.

Submit Your Application: You will need to submit your application and all required documents to a Philippine embassy or consulate. Some types of visas may require an in-person visit, while others might be processed by mail.

Wait for Processing: Once your application is submitted, there will be a processing period. The length of this period can vary, so it is a good idea to apply well in advance of your planned travel dates.

Receive Your Visa: If your application is approved, your visa will be affixed to your passport. Check the details (e.g., validity dates, number of entries) to make sure everything is correct.

It is important to check the specific requirements for your country and visa type, as details can vary. Also, be aware that due to Covid-19, there may be additional requirements or changes to the visa application process.

Remember that the granting of a visa is at the discretion of the consulate or embassy. Always check the latest and detailed information from official resources and consider consulting with a legal expert if needed.

Renewal and long-term stay considerations

If you plan to stay in the Philippines long-term, there are various factors to consider, especially concerning visa renewal and extensions, as well as other aspects of settling into life in the Philippines.

Always ensure you are following legal processes and seek advice from legal professionals or official government sources if you are unsure. Remember, regulations and processes can change, so keep up to date with the latest information.

Visa Renewal and Extensions:
If you are in the Philippines on a tourist visa, you can extend it at the Bureau of Immigration (BI). The initial visa is usually valid for 30 days and can be extended for an additional 59 days. After this, visas can typically be extended further in increments of 1, 2, or 6 months, up to a total stay of 36 months (3 years) for most nationalities.

For long-term stays, consider visas like the Special Resident Retiree's Visa (SRRV) or the Quota Immigrant Visa, which do not require frequent renewals. However, these visas have more stringent requirements.

Proof of Financial Stability:
To renew your visa or apply for certain types of long-term visas, you may need to prove your financial stability. This might involve showing bank statements, proof of income, or evidence of investment in the Philippines.

Accommodation:
For a long-term stay, you will need to consider your housing options. Renting is common, but if you intend to stay for a very long time, you might consider buying property (note that land ownership is generally restricted to Philippine citizens, but foreigners can often own condominium units).

Healthcare:
Ensure that you have a plan for healthcare. Some expats may qualify for PhilHealth, the national health insurance. Alternatively, you might want to look into private health insurance options.

Taxes:
Long-term residents may have tax obligations in the Philippines. Make sure you understand what taxes you may be liable for and how to pay them.

Integration into the Community:
Learning the language and customs, making connections, and participating in local events can make your long-term stay more enjoyable and fulfilling.

Employment and Business:
If you are planning to work or start a business, ensure you have the proper permissions and meet all legal requirements.

Education:
If you have children, you will need to investigate schooling options. There are various international schools that teach foreign curricula if that is what you prefer.

Requirements for permanent residency and citizenship

Permanent Residency

Several pathways can lead to permanent residency in the Philippines, one of which is by obtaining a Special Resident Retiree's Visa (SRRV). This visa is issued to foreign nationals who are at least 35 years old and can make a required deposit in a Philippine bank (the deposit amount varies depending on the applicant's age and other factors). The SRRV essentially grants permanent residency and allows multiple entries into the country.

Another pathway is through marriage to a Filipino citizen. Foreign spouses of Filipino citizens can apply for a 13A Non-Quota Immigrant Visa, which grants permanent residency.

Other ways include obtaining a Quota Visa (granted to a limited number of applicants per year under a basis of reciprocity with their home country) or certain types of work visas.

Citizenship

Acquiring citizenship is more complex. In general, the Philippines does not offer citizenship through investment or residency alone. The most common pathway is through naturalization, which requires the following:

- Applicants must have lived in the Philippines for a continuous period of at least 10 years.
- Applicants must be of good moral character and believe in the principles outlined in the Philippine Constitution.
- Applicants must be able to speak or write English or Spanish or any one of the principal languages.

- Applicants must own real estate in the Philippines worth not less than 5,000 pesos or have a lucrative trade, profession, or lawful occupation.

- Naturalization in the Philippines involves a judicial process and requires renunciation of your original citizenship, as the Philippines generally does not recognize dual citizenship for naturalized citizens.

Note that the Philippines does recognize dual citizenship for former natural-born citizens of the Philippines who have been naturalized in a foreign country.

Please be aware that the laws governing residency and citizenship can change, and the requirements can vary depending on individual circumstances. It is advisable to consult with an immigration lawyer or contact the Philippines Bureau of Immigration for the most accurate and up-to-date information.

Legal rights and responsibilities

As an expatriate living in the Philippines, you are subject to the country's laws and regulations, and you have certain rights and responsibilities. While this is not an exhaustive list, it provides a general overview:

Legal Rights

Protection by Law: As a foreign national residing in the Philippines, you have the right to be protected by the country's laws. This includes protection against crime, discrimination, and certain personal liberties.

Access to Legal Representation: If accused of a crime, you have the right to legal representation and due process under the law.

Engage in Business: Depending on your visa type, you may have the right to engage in commerce, work, or invest in businesses.

Right to Purchase Property: Foreigners are generally allowed to own buildings and condominium units, but not land (with some exceptions).

Access to Services: You should have access to services like health care, education, public transportation, etc.

Legal Responsibilities

Comply with Visa Regulations: Ensure your visa stays valid and comply with its terms (e.g., working only if permitted to do so).

Obey the Law: As an expatriate, you are expected to follow local laws and regulations. This includes traffic rules, drug laws, employment laws, etc.

Respect Local Customs and Norms: While not always legally required, respecting local customs, traditions, and norms is a part of being a responsible expatriate.

Pay Taxes: Depending on your employment status and length of stay, you may be required to pay certain taxes in the Philippines.

Report Changes: You may be required to report changes in your address, employment, or marital status to the Bureau of Immigration.

Remember that violating local laws or the terms of your visa can result in serious consequences, including fines, imprisonment, and deportation. If you are uncertain about your rights or responsibilities, consider seeking legal advice.

Also, remember that while you are protected by the country's laws, your home country's diplomatic representation (e.g., embassy or consulate) can aid in certain situations, such as if you are a victim of a crime or arrested. However, there are limits to what they can do, and they cannot exempt you from local laws.

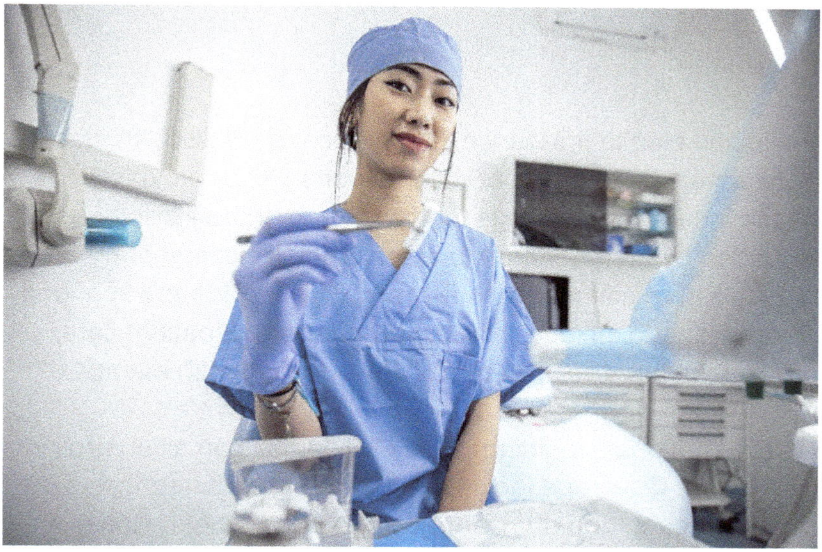

Health and Insurance

Healthcare system in the Philippines

Public Healthcare

The Philippines Department of Health (DOH) is responsible for national health policy, while implementation is carried out at a local level. The public healthcare system is provided by government-run hospitals, healthcare centers, and dispensaries. While the cost of public healthcare is generally low, the quality can vary, particularly between urban and rural areas.

PhilHealth

Philippine Health Insurance Corporation, or PhilHealth, is a government-owned corporation responsible for providing health insurance coverage to the citizens of the Philippines. It is funded by member contributions, and all citizens are required to register. In recent years, PhilHealth has expanded its coverage to include more comprehensive inpatient care, preventive services, and even catastrophic health events.

Foreign nationals residing in the Philippines can also enroll in PhilHealth. Coverage includes hospital stays, surgeries, maternity care, and outpatient care, among others. However, it might not cover all medical costs, and you may need to pay the balance out of pocket.

Private Healthcare

The Philippines also has a robust private healthcare sector, which generally provides a higher standard of care, particularly in major cities. Private hospitals and clinics often have more modern facilities and English-speaking staff. However, the cost is significantly higher than public healthcare.

Many expats and wealthier Filipinos opt for private health insurance to cover these costs. These insurance plans can often be tailored to individual needs and may also provide coverage for treatment abroad.

Pharmacies and Medications

Pharmacies are widely available, particularly in urban areas, and many medications can be purchased directly over the counter. However, the availability of certain medications might be limited, and counterfeit medications can be an issue.

Health Risks

The Philippines has tropical weather, so diseases like dengue fever and malaria can be a concern, especially in certain areas. It is recommended to take appropriate precautions and stay updated on your vaccinations.

In any case, it is advisable to have a good health insurance plan to cover potential health needs while living in the Philippines. Before you move, you should check with your current health insurance provider to see if they offer coverage in the Philippines, or you may need to investigate purchasing a local or international health insurance plan.

Health insurance options (local and international)

Whether you are planning a short-term stay or considering becoming a permanent resident of the Philippines, having health insurance is crucial. There are several local and international options you can consider:

Local Health Insurance Options

Philippine Health Insurance Corporation (PhilHealth): As mentioned earlier, PhilHealth is the national health insurance provider in the Philippines. It covers a significant portion of healthcare costs for many medical conditions and procedures. Expats living and working in the Philippines are eligible to join PhilHealth.

Private Insurance Companies: Several private insurance companies in the Philippines offer a wide range of health insurance products that cover medical expenses, hospitalization, and emergency care. Some of the prominent private health insurance providers include Pacific Cross, Insular Life, and AXA Philippines. These companies offer varying levels of coverage, and the cost depends on factors like age, health condition, and chosen coverage.

International Health Insurance Options

International health insurance plans offer extensive coverage and may include services not covered by local providers. These plans often cover treatment anywhere in the world, which can be beneficial if you travel frequently or want the option of receiving medical treatment in your home country.

Cigna Global: Cigna is one of the most well-known providers of international health insurance. They offer comprehensive coverage and access to a broad network of healthcare providers worldwide.

Aetna International: Aetna is another prominent provider of international health insurance. Their plans also provide extensive coverage and access to a global network of healthcare providers.

Bupa Global: Bupa is a UK-based provider of international health insurance known for its extensive coverage options and global healthcare network.

Allianz Care: Allianz Care offers a range of international health insurance plans tailored to meet different needs, from essential coverage to comprehensive health plans.

Before choosing a health insurance plan, make sure to thoroughly research and compare your options. Consider factors like coverage level, cost, deductible, out-of-pocket maximum, network of healthcare providers, and whether pre-existing conditions are covered.

Vaccinations and preventative care

Taking care of your health while living abroad includes considering preventative measures like vaccinations and routine health checks. Here is what you need to know about vaccinations and preventative care in the Philippines:

Vaccinations:

Before moving to the Philippines, you should ensure your routine vaccinations are up to date. These typically include:

- MMR (Measles, Mumps, Rubella)

- Diphtheria-Tetanus-Pertussis
- Varicella (Chickenpox)
- Polio
- Seasonal flu

According to the U.S. Centers for Disease Control and Prevention (CDC), you should also consider the following vaccinations before moving to or visiting the Philippines:

- Hepatitis A: Recommended for most travelers to protect against foodborne diseases.
- Hepatitis B: Recommended if you might have sex with a new partner, get a tattoo or piercing, or any medical procedures.
- Typhoid: Recommended for most travelers, especially if visiting smaller cities or rural areas.
- Japanese Encephalitis: You may need this vaccine if your trip will last more than a month, depending on where you are going in the Philippines and what time of year you are traveling. You should also consider this vaccine if you plan to visit rural areas in the Philippines or will be spending a lot of time outdoors, even for trips shorter than a month.
- Rabies: Although rabies can be found in dogs, bats, and other mammals in the Philippines, it is not a major risk to most travelers. CDC recommends this vaccine for only these groups: Travelers involved in outdoor and other activities (such as camping, hiking, biking, adventure travel, and caving) that put them at risk for animal bites. People who will be working with or around animals (such as veterinarians, wildlife professionals, and researchers). People

who are taking long trips or moving to the Philippines.

Preventative Care:

Living in a tropical country like the Philippines comes with its own set of health risks. Preventive measures should include:

- Malaria and Dengue: Use insect repellent, wear protective clothing, and stay in accommodations with screens on windows and doors to prevent mosquito bites.
- Food and Water Safety: Only drink water that has been filtered, treated, or boiled, and be careful about eating street food.
- Heat and Sun Exposure: Protect yourself from heat stroke and sunburn by staying hydrated and using sunblock.
- Regular Check-ups: Keep up with regular health check-ups and screenings appropriate for your age and gender.
- Remember to consult with your healthcare provider to determine which vaccinations and preventative measures are right for you based on your health history and the specific areas of the Philippines you plan to visit or live in.

Dealing with medical emergencies

Dealing with a medical emergency in a foreign country can be daunting. Here are some tips and information you should know about handling medical emergencies in the Philippines:

Emergency Services:

The Philippines has a centralized emergency phone number for urgent situations. Dial 911 for immediate emergency assistance.

Hospitals:

The quality of healthcare can vary in the Philippines. In major cities, there are private hospitals and clinics that offer high-quality healthcare and have English-speaking staff. However, in rural or remote areas, the standard of healthcare facilities might not be as high, and access to specialized care can be limited.

Some of the highly regarded hospitals in Manila, the capital city, are the Asian Hospital and Medical Center, St. Luke's Medical Center, and the Makati Medical Center.

Insurance:

Ensure that your health insurance plan covers emergency medical evacuation, especially if you plan to live in or visit remote areas. Medical evacuation can be expensive but crucial if you are in an area where the necessary medical facilities are not available.

First Aid:

Having a basic understanding of first aid can be invaluable during a medical emergency. It is beneficial to know how to perform CPR and how to manage other health crises until professional medical help arrives.

Prescriptions:

If you are on prescription medication, make sure to bring enough with you, and keep a copy of your prescription. While many medications can be purchased directly from pharmacies in the Philippines, the availability of certain medications might be limited.

Medical Alert ID:

If you have a chronic condition or serious allergy, consider wearing a medical alert bracelet or necklace. This can communicate critical information to first responders in an emergency.

Emergency Contacts:

Always have a list of emergency contacts at hand. This should include your next of kin, your country's embassy or consulate in the Philippines, your healthcare provider, and your insurance company.

While this advice can help you be better prepared, it is crucial to seek immediate medical attention in an emergency. Always consult a healthcare professional for any health concerns.

Housing and Accommodation

Renting vs. buying

Choosing between renting and buying a home is a significant decision when moving to the Philippines, and it will depend on various factors, including your financial situation, how long you plan to stay, and your personal preferences. Here are some things to consider:

Renting:

Pros:

- **Flexibility**: Renting can be a good option if you are unsure of your long-term plans or if your job requires you to be mobile.
- **Lower Initial Costs**: Renting usually involves lower initial costs than buying a house, which requires a substantial down payment. Renting only requires a security deposit and advance rent.
- **Less Responsibility**: Renters do not have to worry about maintenance or repairs, which are typically the landlord's responsibility.
- **Ease of Changing Accommodations**: If your circumstances change or you are not happy with your current location, you can more easily move.

Cons:

- **No Equity**: When you rent, you are not building equity, as you would when paying a mortgage.
- **Rent Increases**: The cost of rent can increase over time, whereas a fixed-rate mortgage would not.
- **Less Control**: As a renter, you have less control over the property. There may be restrictions on pets, renovations, and other aspects of living in the property.

Buying:

Pros:

- **Building Equity**: When you buy a home, you are building equity. This can be financially beneficial in the long run.
- **Stability**: Owning a home offers a sense of stability and can be particularly appealing to those with families or those planning to stay in one place for a long time.
- **More Control**: As a homeowner, you have more freedom to customize your living space.

Cons:

- **Higher Initial Costs**: Buying a home requires a significant upfront investment, including a down payment, closing costs, and other expenses.
- **Maintenance Responsibilities**: As a homeowner, you are responsible for all maintenance and repairs.
- **Less Mobility**: Selling a home can take time, which might not be ideal if you need to move quickly for a job or other reasons.

It is important to note that foreign ownership of land is generally not allowed in the Philippines. However, foreigners can own condominium units as long as 60% of the condo corporation is owned by Filipinos. This is one reason why many expats choose to rent rather than buy.

Typical housing cost

Renting:

In Metro Manila, which includes the capital city of Manila and surrounding cities like Makati and Quezon City, you can expect the following rental prices:

- For a one-bedroom apartment in the city center, rent can range from 20,000 to 50,000 PHP per month (roughly $400 - $1,000 USD).
- In less central areas, a one-bedroom might cost between 10,000 to 20,000 PHP per month (roughly $200 - $400 USD).
- Larger apartments or houses will cost significantly more, especially in high-end areas.
- In other major cities like Cebu City or Davao City, rents are generally less expensive than in Metro Manila.

Buying:

The cost of buying property also varies widely:

- In Manila's city center, the price per square meter for an apartment could range from 150,000 to 300,000 PHP (roughly $3,000 - $6,000 USD).
- Outside the city center, prices might be in the range of 40,000 to 70,000 PHP per square meter (roughly $800 - $1,400 USD). Again, property prices in other cities are generally lower than in Manila.

Other Costs:

Do not forget about other housing-related costs. If you are renting, you will also need to budget for utilities such as electricity, water, and internet. If you are buying, there will be costs for property taxes, maintenance, and possibly homeowners association fees.

In terms of purchasing property, as a reminder, foreign nationals generally can't own land in the Philippines (though they can own buildings and units, such as in a condominium, subject to certain restrictions).

Before deciding, make sure to conduct thorough research, visit potential homes in person, and consult with real estate professionals to understand the current housing market conditions in the Philippines.

Choosing a location

Choosing a location in the Philippines will depend on several factors such as your lifestyle preferences, work commitments, budget, and family needs. Here are some factors to consider when choosing a location:

Cost of Living: The cost of living varies considerably across the Philippines. Generally, it is higher in major cities like Manila and Cebu compared to smaller cities and rural areas. Manila, Makati, and Bonifacio Global City are among the most expensive places to live, while there are less expensive options in the outlying cities and provinces.

Lifestyle: If you enjoy a fast-paced, urban lifestyle with amenities such as shopping centers, restaurants, nightlife, and cultural activities, a major city like Manila or Cebu might be a good fit. On the other hand, if you prefer a quieter, more relaxed lifestyle, you might consider living in provinces such as Palawan or Bohol, known for their natural beauty and laid-back lifestyle.

Work: If you are moving to the Philippines for work, the location of your job will be a significant factor. Traffic in major cities like Manila can be heavy, so living close to your workplace can save you a lot of commuting time.

Safety and Infrastructure: Consider the safety of the area, as well as the availability of essential infrastructure like reliable electricity, clean water, and internet connectivity.

Community: Some expats prefer to live in areas with a large foreign community. In the Philippines, there are significant expat communities in places like Makati City, Taguig City, Cebu City, and Angeles City.

Family Needs: If you are moving with your family, you will want to consider the availability of good schools, family-friendly recreational facilities, and safe neighborhoods.

Healthcare Facilities: Access to good healthcare is crucial, especially in case of emergencies. Proximity to reputable hospitals and clinics is an important consideration.

Climate: The Philippines is a tropical country and is warm year-round. However, some areas in high elevations like Baguio City, known as the "Summer Capital of the Philippines," have a cooler climate.

Visiting the Philippines and exploring different areas before you decide where to live can be very helpful. It allows you to get a feel for the different regions and what they have to offer and can help you make the best decision based on your personal preferences and needs.

Utilities and other expenses

Utilities:

Electricity: The cost of electricity in the Philippines is higher than in many other countries due to the country's dependence on imported fuel. On average, a monthly bill for an 85m2 (915ft2) apartment might range from PHP 3,500 to PHP 10,000 ($70-$200), depending on your usage and the efficiency of your appliances. Air conditioning, which is often necessary in the hot climate, can significantly increase these costs.

Water: The cost of water is usually less than electricity. A monthly bill might range from PHP 200 to PHP 500 ($4-$10).

Internet: The cost of the internet in the Philippines can vary depending on the provider and plan. On average, you might expect to pay between PHP 1,500 to PHP 3,000 ($30-$60) per month for a broadband connection.

Mobile Phone: The cost of a mobile phone plan can range from PHP 300 to PHP 1,000 ($6-$20) per month, depending on the provider and plan. Prepaid plans are also common in the Philippines.

Other Expenses:

Food: The cost of food will depend on your lifestyle and whether you prefer to cook at home, eat out, or a mix of both. A monthly grocery bill for a single person might be around PHP 3,000 to PHP 5,000 ($60-$100), while a meal at an inexpensive restaurant might cost around PHP 150 to PHP 300 ($3-$6).

Transportation: Public transportation is relatively cheap in the Philippines. A one-way ticket on local transport might cost around PHP 20 ($0.40), while a monthly pass might be around PHP 1,000 ($20). Taxi starts rates begin at around PHP 40 ($0.80), with an additional PHP 13-15 ($0.26-$0.30) per kilometer. Owning a car comes with additional costs for gasoline, maintenance, and parking.

Leisure Activities: Costs for activities like going to the cinema, gym membership, or dining out can vary. For example, a monthly gym membership might cost between PHP 1,000 to PHP 2,500 ($20-$50), and a cinema ticket might cost around PHP 200-300 ($4-$6).

Household Help: It is common in the Philippines for families to hire household help such as maids, drivers, and gardeners. The cost can vary, but a full-time live-in maid might earn a salary of around PHP 3,000 to PHP 5,000 ($60-$100) per month.

These are average costs and actual costs can vary widely based on lifestyle, location, and personal consumption.

Cost of Living

Typical monthly expenses

The cost of living in the Philippines can vary significantly based on your lifestyle, location, and personal preferences. However, as a guideline, here are some typical monthly expenses you might expect:

Here is a single person's average monthly budget example from an expat living in Dumaguete 4/1/2023.

Rent 1 Bedroom Apartment	236
Utilities	16
Grocery	25
Doctors Office	90
Laundry	5
Entertainment/Eating Out	212
Transport Rent/Oil Change	41
Visa	35
TOTAL	**$660 USD**

Here is a single person's Cebu City average monthly budget 6/1/2023.

Rent 2 Bedroom Apartment	1,000
Utilities	250
Groceries	500
Transportation	50
Entertainment	400
TOTAL	**$2,200 USD**

Housing: Rent for a one-bedroom apartment in a city center might range from PHP 20,000 to PHP 50,000 ($400-$1,000), while outside the city center it could be between PHP 10,000 to PHP 20,000 ($200-$400). The cost can significantly increase for larger apartments or houses, particularly in upscale neighborhoods.

Utilities: This includes electricity, water, heating, cooling, and garbage. For an 85m2 apartment, you might expect to pay around PHP 3,500 to PHP 10,000 ($70-$200) per month.

Internet: A monthly bill might be between PHP 1,500 to PHP 3,000 ($30-$60).

Mobile Phone: Depending on your plan, this might cost between PHP 300 to PHP 1,000 ($6-$20) per month.

Food: If you cook at home, a monthly grocery bill might be around PHP 3,000 to PHP 5,000 ($60-$100). Eating out occasionally will increase this cost.

Transportation: If you use public transport, a monthly pass might cost around PHP 1,000 ($20). If you own a car, you will have additional costs for gasoline, maintenance, and possibly parking.

Health Insurance: The cost can vary widely based on your coverage. For private health insurance, you might expect to pay anywhere from PHP 1,500 to PHP 5,000 ($30-$100) per month.

Leisure Activities: Depending on your lifestyle, you might budget for costs such as dining out, gym membership, cinema tickets, and other activities.

Household Help: If you choose to hire help such as a maid or driver, a full-time live-in maid might earn a salary of around PHP 3,000 to PHP 5,000 ($60-$100) per month.

These are broad estimates and actual costs can vary. It is also worth considering unexpected costs and setting aside some money for emergencies. Additionally, if you have children, you will have to factor in costs such as schooling and childcare.

Cost of food and groceries

The cost of food and groceries in the Philippines can vary significantly depending on your dietary habits, where you shop, and whether you are in a city or a more rural area.

Rice: As a staple of the Filipino diet, rice is relatively inexpensive. A kilogram of rice might cost around PHP 40-50 ($0.80-$1).

Chicken: A kilogram of chicken might cost around PHP 140-170 ($2.80-$3.40).

Beef: A kilogram of beef could be around PHP 300-400 ($6-$8).

Fish: Fish is a common part of the diet in the Philippines. A kilogram might cost around PHP 200-300 ($4-$6), depending on the type of fish.

Fruits and Vegetables: Prices can vary depending on the season and type of produce. For example, a kilogram of bananas might be around PHP 60-80 ($1.20-$1.60), and a kilogram of tomatoes might be around PHP 60-100 ($1.20-$2).

Bread: A loaf of fresh white bread might cost around PHP 50-60 ($1-$1.20).

Milk: A liter of milk might cost around PHP 80-100 ($1.60-$2).

Eating Out: A meal at an inexpensive restaurant might cost around PHP 150-200 ($3-$4), while a three-course meal for two people at a mid-range restaurant might cost around PHP 700-1,500 ($14-$30).

Fast Food: A combo meal at a fast-food restaurant like McDonald's or Jollibee might cost around PHP 150-200 ($3-$4).

These are average prices and can vary. Imported goods, organic products, or specialty items are likely to be more expensive. Shopping at local markets can often be cheaper than supermarkets, and haggling is common practice.

Keep in mind that food expenses can be one of the most flexible parts of your budget. By adjusting your eating habits — such as eating at home more often, buying in-season produce, or choosing local goods instead of imported ones — you can significantly affect your monthly expenses.

Cost of transportation

Transportation costs in the Philippines will vary based on your preferred mode of transportation and the frequency of your travel. Here are some average costs for transportation in the Philippines:

Public Transport: Public transportation in the Philippines is relatively cheap. A one-way ticket on local transport like jeepneys or buses might cost around PHP 15-25 ($0.30-$0.50). For frequent travelers, a monthly pass might be around PHP 1,000 ($20).

Taxis and Rideshares: The start rate for taxis is typically around PHP 40 ($0.80), with an additional PHP 13-15 ($0.26-$0.30) per kilometer. Rideshare services like Grab are also popular and have similar costs, but prices can surge during peak times or severe weather.

Private Vehicle: If you own a car, you will need to consider the costs of gasoline, maintenance, and parking. Gasoline prices are PHP 50-60 ($1-$1.20) per liter. Car maintenance costs can vary widely but budgeting around PHP 10,000-20,000 ($200-$400) per year might be a starting point.

Bicycles and Motorcycles: Bicycles and motorcycles are popular means of transportation in the Philippines, especially in less congested areas. The cost of a new bicycle can range from PHP 5,000-15,000 ($100-$300), while a new motorcycle can cost PHP 40,000-80,000 ($800-$1,600) or more, depending on the model.

Car Rentals: If you prefer to rent a car occasionally, the cost can vary depending on the type of car and duration of rental, but you might expect to pay PHP 2,000-3,000 ($40-$60) per day.

Tricycles and Pedicabs: In smaller towns and for shorter distances, tricycles (motorcycles with sidecars) and pedicabs (bicycle version) are common. A ride might cost PHP 10-20 ($0.20-$0.40).

Remember, transportation costs can fluctuate based on fuel prices, route, time of day, and other factors. Walking or cycling for short distances not only saves money but is also good for health and the environment. If you are planning to use public transport frequently, getting familiar with the routes and learning the local systems can help you travel more efficiently.

Leisure and entertainment costs

Leisure and entertainment costs in the Philippines can vary widely depending on your interests and lifestyle. Here are some average costs you might expect:

Dining Out: A meal at an inexpensive restaurant might cost around PHP 150-200 ($3-$4), while a three-course meal for two people at a mid-range restaurant might be around PHP 700-1,500 ($14-$30).

Cinema: A movie ticket might cost around PHP 200-300 ($4-$6).

Gym Membership: A monthly gym membership in a city might cost between PHP 1,000 to PHP 2,500 ($20-$50).

Sports: Renting a tennis court for an hour might cost around PHP 200-500 ($4-$10). Golf is also popular, though more expensive, with green fees at a mid-range course possibly ranging from PHP 1,000-2,500 ($20-$50).

Outdoor Activities: The Philippines has many opportunities for outdoor activities. Entrance fees for national parks or nature reserves might range from PHP 50-300 ($1-$6). Activities like scuba diving or island-hopping tours can be more expensive, possibly ranging from PHP 1,000-3,000 ($20-$60).

Nightlife: Prices for nightlife can vary widely. A local beer at a bar might cost PHP 50-100 ($1-$2), while cocktails or imported drinks can be more expensive. Cover charges for clubs can vary but might be around PHP 300-500 ($6-$10), sometimes including a drink.

Cultural Activities: Entrance fees for museums or cultural sites typically range from PHP 100-300 ($2-$6). Shows, concerts, or other live performances can have a wide range of ticket prices depending on the event.

Travel: The Philippines is an archipelago with many islands, and travel between them can be a significant cost. A domestic flight might cost PHP 1,000-3,000 ($20-$60), and a ferry ride might be PHP 200-1,000 ($4-$20). Accommodation, food, and activities during travel will add to this cost.

These are average costs, and actual costs can vary widely based on personal preferences and lifestyle. Remember, leisure and entertainment costs are discretionary and can be adjusted based on your budget. It is also worth noting that there are many free or low-cost activities available, like enjoying the country's beautiful beaches, hiking, or exploring local markets and neighborhoods.

Education

Overview of the education system

The education system in the Philippines is managed by the Department of Education for basic education, and the Commission on Higher Education for tertiary and graduate education. The Technical Education and Skills Development Authority (TESDA) administers middle-level education training and development.

Here is an overview of the system:

Early Childhood Education (Pre-school): While not compulsory, pre-school education is available for children aged 3-5 years. This level is further divided into Kindergarten and Preparatory stages.

Basic Education (K-12 Program): As of 2012, the Philippines implemented the K-12 Program, which covers 13 years of basic education. This is divided into:

Kindergarten
Elementary School (Grade 1-6)
Junior High School (Grade 7-10)
Senior High School (Grade 11-12): This is where students choose their career tracks. Tracks include: Academic, Technical-Vocational-Livelihood, Sports, and Arts and Design.
Higher Education: After finishing Grade 12, students may choose to pursue higher education, which includes:

Undergraduate studies: Students can earn bachelor's degrees, which usually take 4 years.
Graduate studies: This includes master's programs, Doctorate programs, and post-Doctorate programs.
Technical and Vocational Education and Training (TVET): For those who want to develop their skills but do not want to go through college, they can enroll in vocational courses offered by TESDA. These programs provide practical skills and knowledge needed for specific jobs.

It is worth noting that the medium of instruction in the Philippine education system is English, making it one of the top English-speaking countries in Asia. However, Filipino (based on Tagalog) and local languages are also used, particularly in the early years of elementary education.

International schools are widely available for expatriates or those wanting an international curriculum, but these can be quite expensive. There are also private and public schools available. Public schools are state-funded and offer free education, while private schools are funded by tuition fees and other school fees. The quality of education can vary significantly from school to school, so it is recommended to thoroughly research options when choosing a school.

International and local schools

The Philippines offers a range of educational choices for both local and foreign students, including local public schools, private schools, and international schools. These options can differ in terms of curriculum, language of instruction, cost, and overall approach to education.

Local Public Schools:

Funded by the government, public schools provide free education to Filipino citizens.
Classes are typically conducted in Filipino and English.
They follow the K-12 curriculum mandated by the Department of Education.

Local Private Schools:

They are funded by tuition fees and may offer a higher quality of education compared to public schools.
Most private schools follow the same K-12 curriculum but may provide additional programs or courses. Some private schools offer unique curriculums, such as Montessori or Waldorf education.

They may offer smaller class sizes, more extracurricular activities, and better facilities compared to public schools.

International Schools:

International schools in the Philippines primarily cater to expatriate students, though they also accept local students. They follow an international curriculum, such as the International Baccalaureate (IB) or the curriculum of specific countries like the U.S., UK, Canada, or Australia. This can be beneficial for families who move frequently between countries, as it provides continuity in education. English is typically the medium of instruction, but some schools may offer instruction in other languages depending on their affiliation. They often have diverse student bodies, offering students the opportunity to interact with peers from various cultural backgrounds.

International schools tend to have higher tuition fees compared to local schools. They typically offer high-quality education, modern facilities, a wide range of extracurricular activities, and smaller student-to-teacher ratios. When choosing a school, it is important to consider the child's needs and plans. For instance, a family planning to stay long-term in the Philippines might choose a local school, while a family expecting to move back to their home country, or another country might choose an international school. It is also important to visit schools, talk to administrators and teachers, and consider the school's location, reputation, and the experiences of other students and parents.

Schooling options for expat children

Expatriate families living in the Philippines have several schooling options for their children. These include international schools, private local schools, and homeschooling.

International Schools:

International schools are often the most popular choice for expat families as they offer a global curriculum and are taught mainly in English. Some of these schools follow the International Baccalaureate (IB) curriculum, while others may follow the curriculum of a specific country such as the American, British, or Australian curriculum.

Advantages of international schools can include:

- Continuity of education, especially for families who move frequently.
- Diverse student population.
- High educational standards and modern facilities.
- Extracurricular activities that might not be available in local schools.
- Some notable international schools in the Philippines include the International School Manila, British School Manila, and Brent International School Manila.

Private Local Schools:

Some expat families choose to enroll their children in private local schools. These schools follow the Philippine curriculum, and although the mode of instruction is English, Filipino is taught as a subject and sometimes used as a medium of instruction as well.

Advantages can include:

- Lower tuition fees compared to international schools.
- Greater immersion in local culture and language.
- Variety of private schools with different educational approaches (like Montessori or Waldorf schools).

Homeschooling:

Homeschooling is another option that some expat families in the Philippines choose. This is a legal and increasingly popular option in the country.

Advantages can include:

- Flexibility in curriculum and schedule.
- The ability to tailor the education experience to the child's individual needs.
- More control over the child's learning environment.
- There are homeschooling organizations that can provide support, such as the Homeschool Association of the Philippine Islands (HAPI).

Remember, choosing the right school depends on your child's individual needs, your family's plans (like potential future relocations), and your personal values and preferences. It is a good idea to research thoroughly, visit potential schools, and speak with other expat parents to get their insights and experiences.

Adult and continuing education opportunities

In the Philippines, there are numerous opportunities for adults to continue their education or enhance their skills, either for personal enrichment or for professional advancement. Here are some options:

Universities and Colleges:
Many universities and colleges in the Philippines offer graduate programs, including master's and doctoral degrees, in a variety of fields. Some institutions also offer certificate programs and short courses designed for working professionals. Additionally, there are Open University systems, like the one from the University of the Philippines, that offer flexible distance learning programs.

Technical and Vocational Education and Training (TVET):
The Technical Education and Skills Development Authority (TESDA) offers a wide range of vocational courses in fields like agriculture, automotive, electronics, and information technology. TESDA courses often provide practical skills and certifications that can help individuals advance in their careers or start new ones.

Language Classes:
Language schools and cultural institutes offer classes for adults who want to learn a new language. English language courses are particularly popular, but classes in other languages, like Mandarin, Japanese, Spanish, and Filipino, are also available.

Online Learning Platforms:
Online learning platforms like Coursera, edX, Udemy, and LinkedIn Learning provide a wide variety of courses on many subjects, allowing individuals to learn at their own pace. Topics can range from business and technology to art and personal development.

Community Education:
Some local community centers and libraries offer workshops or classes for adults. These may include topics like art, music, cooking, computer literacy, personal finance, and health and wellness.

Professional Development:
Many industries have professional organizations that offer training seminars, workshops, and certification programs. Companies may also provide continuing education opportunities for their employees.

Before choosing an adult or continuing education program, it is important to consider your goals, interests, schedule, and budget. Additionally, for professional advancement, it can be beneficial to consider the demand for certain skills or credentials in your industry.

Work and Business

Employment opportunities and job market overview

The job market in the Philippines is diverse and rapidly evolving, thanks to its growing economy and strategic location in Southeast Asia. While the opportunities can vary depending on your industry and skillset, here is a general overview of the employment opportunities and job market in the Philippines:

Growing Industries:

Information Technology and Business Process Management (IT-BPM): This sector, which includes call centers, IT services, and other outsourcing services, is one of the largest and fastest-growing industries in the country. Opportunities are particularly strong for roles in IT support, software development, customer service, and business operations.

Electronics and Semiconductors: The Philippines is a significant player in the global semiconductor and electronics industry, offering opportunities in manufacturing, engineering, and related roles.

Healthcare: With a rapidly growing and aging population, there are opportunities in healthcare, including nursing, pharmacy, physical therapy, and healthcare administration.

Tourism and Hospitality: This industry plays a significant role in the country's economy, offering opportunities in hotels, resorts, travel agencies, and related businesses.

Finance: As the economy grows, so does demand for financial services, creating opportunities in banking, insurance, financial planning, and related areas.

Real Estate and Construction: The country's robust economic growth and urban development have driven demand for professionals in real estate and construction.

Job Search:

Online Job Portals: Websites like JobStreet, Kalibrr, and LinkedIn are popular platforms for job searching in the Philippines. They list thousands of job opportunities across a wide range of industries.

Networking: Networking can be very effective, particularly in certain industries. Expats might start with their home country's chamber of commerce or other business groups in the Philippines.

Recruitment Agencies: These can be helpful, especially for higher-level positions or specialized roles.

Working Legally: Remember, to work legally in the Philippines, foreigners typically need a work visa or permit. The specific requirements can vary depending on the type of job and other factors.

Final Thoughts: While the Philippines offers many opportunities, it is also a competitive job market, and it is important to be aware of the challenges. These can include lower salaries compared to Western countries, cultural differences, and in some cases, restrictions on foreign workers in certain roles or industries. It is essential to do thorough research and possibly seek local legal advice when considering employment in the Philippines.

Starting a business in the Philippines

Starting a business in the Philippines, as in any country, requires careful planning, a clear understanding of the business environment, and compliance with numerous regulatory procedures. Below is an outline of the steps required:

1. **Identify Your Business Type and Structure**: Decide if your business will be a sole proprietorship, partnership, corporation, or a branch office. Each business type has different requirements, regulations, and limitations, especially for foreign owners.
2. **Register Your Business Name**: The Department of Trade and Industry (DTI) handles the registration of business names for sole proprietorships. For partnerships and corporations, the Securities and Exchange Commission (SEC) is responsible.
3. **Prepare and File Articles of Incorporation (for Corporations) or Partnership (for Partnerships)**: This step involves providing details about the business, its purpose, and the people involved. This document is submitted to the SEC.
4. **Obtain Barangay Clearance**: This is issued by the local Barangay (the smallest administrative division in the Philippines) where the business is located. It is a basic requirement for the issuance of the Business Permit or Mayor's Permit.
5. **Obtain Mayor's Permit or Business Permit**: This is issued by the local municipality where the business is located. The process and requirements can vary depending on the city or municipality.

6. **Register with the Bureau of Internal Revenue (BIR)**: This step involves getting a taxpayer identification number (TIN), registering your books of accounts, getting invoices and receipts printed and approved, and paying the annual registration fee.
7. **Register with Relevant Government Agencies**: Depending on the nature of your business and your employees, you may also need to register with the Social Security System (SSS), the Philippine Health Insurance Corporation (PhilHealth), and the Home Development Mutual Fund (Pag-IBIG Fund).
8. **Obtain Other Necessary Permits and Licenses**: Depending on the nature of your business, other permits and licenses may be required. For instance, you might need a permit from the Food and Drug Administration (FDA) if you are starting a food or drug business, or from the Department of Labor and Employment (DOLE) if you will be hiring employees.

When starting a business in the Philippines, it is advisable to engage with a local lawyer or business consultant who can guide you through the entire process, ensure that you comply with all legal requirements, and advise you on how to navigate the local business culture. Doing so will help you avoid costly mistakes and maximize your chances of success.

Labor laws and employee rights

In the Philippines, labor laws and employee rights are governed by the Labor Code of the Philippines, a statute that prescribes the rules and regulations for employment practices and relations. The Department of Labor and Employment

(DOLE) oversees and enforces these regulations. Here are key points:

Standard Work Hours and Overtime: The standard workweek in the Philippines is 48 hours, typically broken down into six 8-hour workdays. Employees who work beyond 8 hours a day are entitled to overtime pay.

Rest Days and Holidays: Employees are generally entitled to at least one rest day per week. There are several regular and special non-working holidays in the Philippines where employees receive premium pay if they work.

Minimum Wage: The minimum wage in the Philippines varies by region, sector, and industry. It is set by the Regional Tripartite Wages and Productivity Boards.

13th Month Pay: Employees in the Philippines are entitled to a 13th-month pay, which is a mandatory bonus equivalent to one month's salary, payable in December.

Maternity and Paternity Leave: Female employees are entitled to 105 days of paid maternity leave for live childbirth, regardless of the mode of delivery, and regardless of how many times such childbirth occurs. Male employees, on the other hand, are entitled to seven days of paid paternity leave for the first four deliveries of his legitimate spouse.

Retirement Pay: Employees who have served at least five years in a company are entitled to retirement pay, equivalent to at least half a month's salary for every year of service.

Termination and Severance Pay: Employers must have a just or authorized cause to terminate an employee. In cases of legal termination, employees may be entitled to separation or severance pay.

Social Security: Employers must contribute to the Social Security System (SSS), Philippine Health Insurance Corporation (PhilHealth), and Home Development Mutual Fund (Pag-IBIG Fund) on behalf of their employees.

Health and Safety: Employers are required to maintain safe and healthy workplaces for their employees and are required to comply with occupational health and safety standards.

Remember that these are general guidelines, and certain industries may have specific regulations or exceptions. It is advisable for employers, especially those from other countries, to seek legal advice to ensure they fully understand and comply with Philippine labor laws.

Income tax considerations

Tax laws in the Philippines can be quite complex and may change over time, so it is crucial to consult with a tax advisor or accountant who is familiar with the local tax regulations. Here are some general points to consider about income tax in the Philippines:

Residency Status: Your tax obligations in the Philippines will depend on your residency status. Residents and citizens are taxed on their worldwide income, while non-residents are only taxed on their income from sources within the Philippines.

Tax Rates: The Philippines has a progressive tax system for individuals, with rates ranging from 0% to 35%. For corporations, the standard corporate income tax rate is 30%.

Taxable Income: Taxable income includes earnings from employment, business profits, and passive income such as rent, dividends, and interest. Some types of income, such as certain fringe benefits, may be subject to different tax rules.

Deductions and Exemptions: The Philippines allows certain deductions and exemptions that can lower your taxable income. For example, there are deductions for business expenses, personal exemptions for individuals, and additional exemptions for dependents.

Filing and Payment: Income tax returns in the Philippines are generally due on or before April 15 of the following year. The Bureau of Internal Revenue (BIR) has an Electronic Filing and Payment System (eFPS) for online filing and payment.

Double Taxation Treaties: The Philippines has double taxation treaties with several countries, which can help prevent you from being taxed on the same income in both the Philippines and your home country.

Value-Added Tax (VAT): The standard rate is 12%, and this applies to most goods and services. Some items are zero-rated or exempt from VAT.

Remember, these are only general considerations and may not cover all potential tax obligations. It is always advisable to consult with a tax professional or legal advisor to understand your specific tax situation when moving to a new country.

Language and Culture

Local languages (Tagalog and English)

The Philippines is a multilingual country with over 170 languages spoken across its islands. The country has two official languages: Filipino (based on Tagalog) and English.

Filipino/Tagalog: Filipino, which is largely based on Tagalog, is the national language of the Philippines. It is the first language of the country's capital, Manila, and several surrounding provinces. Most Filipinos are bilingual and can speak Filipino alongside their regional language. Although Filipino is based on Tagalog, it incorporates words and phrases from other Philippine languages.

English: English is also widely spoken and understood in the Philippines due to the country's history as a former U.S. colony and the continued use of English in government, business, law, education, and media. In fact, the Philippines is one of the largest English-speaking countries in the world by the number of speakers. Most Filipinos are taught English as a second language from a young age in school.

Regional Languages: The Philippines is home to a multitude of regional languages and dialects. Cebuano, also known as Bisaya or Visayan, is widely spoken in the Visayas and Mindanao regions. Other regional languages include Ilokano, Hiligaynon (another Visayan language), Waray-Waray, Kapampangan, and more.

If you are planning to move to the Philippines, you will find that being able to communicate in English will be highly beneficial. However, learning some Filipino (Tagalog) can help you integrate better into the local culture and can be appreciated by the locals.

Cultural norms and etiquette

Filipino culture is a unique blend of Eastern and Western influences, stemming from the country's indigenous heritage, Spanish colonial history, American occupation, and Asian influences. Here are some key cultural norms and etiquette to be aware of:

Respect for Elders: Filipinos demonstrate respect for elders by using polite forms of address, like "po" and "opo," and through the traditional "mano," where younger individuals take an elder's hand and press it to their forehead as a sign of respect. Always use "sir" or "ma'am" when addressing someone older or in a position of authority.

Hospitality: Filipinos are renowned for their hospitality. It is common for hosts to insist guests eat or accept refreshments. Declining may be seen as impolite.

Religion: The Philippines is predominantly Roman Catholic, and religion plays a significant role in people's lives. Respect religious customs and practices, including attending Mass on Sundays, observing local festivals, and respecting religious icons.

Punctuality: While punctuality is appreciated, Filipinos may have a more relaxed sense of time compared to Western standards, often referred to as "Filipino time". However, for business meetings and formal events, it is generally expected to be on time.

Social Graces: It is customary to smile and make small talk. Direct eye contact is important as a sign of sincerity and honesty.

Group Harmony ("Pakikisama"): Filipinos place a high value on smooth interpersonal relationships and group harmony. They may go to great lengths to avoid offending others, even to the point of downplaying their own desires or opinions. Try to avoid confrontational behavior or causing others to "lose face."

Communication Style: Filipinos often communicate indirectly to avoid confrontation and maintain harmony. Non-verbal communication is also crucial, so pay attention to body language, tone of voice, and context.

Dining Etiquette: When invited to a Filipino home for a meal, it is polite to bring a small gift for the host. Wait for the host to invite you to start eating. It is also polite to finish everything on your plate.

Dress Code: Filipinos generally dress modestly, and this is particularly important in rural areas and places of worship. In business settings, attire is typically formal.

Remember that cultural norms can vary by region, city, and individual, so it is essential to maintain an open mind and be observant of local customs and behaviors. Always demonstrate respect for local culture, traditions, and practices.

Holidays and festivals

The Philippines, known as the "Fiesta Islands," celebrates numerous holidays and festivals throughout the year, many of which are based on religious traditions, historical events, and local customs. Here are some of the most significant ones:

New Year's Day (January 1): The start of the new year is a public holiday and is celebrated with fireworks and family gatherings.

Araw ng Kagitingan (Day of Valor, April 9): This is a national holiday commemorating the fall of Bataan during World War II.

Holy Week (March/April): This is one of the most important observances in this predominantly Catholic country. It starts on Palm Sunday and culminates on Easter Sunday. Good Friday and Black Saturday are public holidays. Maundy Thursday is also a public holiday where Filipinos typically visit several churches in a practice known as "Visita Iglesia."

Independence Day (June 12): This commemorates the Philippines' declaration of independence from Spain in 1898.

National Heroes Day (Last Monday of August): This holiday honors the country's national heroes.

Bonifacio Day (November 30): This holiday commemorates the birth of Andres Bonifacio, a national hero who played a significant role in the struggle for independence from Spain.

Christmas (December 25): The Philippines is known for having one of the longest Christmas seasons in the world, starting as early as September and extending until early January. Christmas Day itself is a public holiday and is celebrated with family gatherings, masses, and festive meals.

Rizal Day (December 30): This holiday commemorates the execution of the national hero, Dr. Jose Rizal, who was a key figure in the Philippine Revolution against Spanish rule.

In addition to these national holidays, there are many vibrant and colorful local festivals ("fiestas") held throughout the year, including:

Ati-Atihan (Kalibo, January): A festival in honor of the Santo Niño (Infant Jesus), featuring tribal dance, music, and indigenous costumes.

Sinulog (Cebu City, January): Another festival in honor of the Santo Niño, celebrated with a grand parade, street dancing, and festive decorations.

Panagbenga (Baguio, February): Known as the "Flower Festival," this event features float parades, street dancing, and exhibitions.

Pahiyas (Lucban, May): A colorful and creative harvest festival where locals decorate their homes with produce and farm products.

Remember that many businesses and government offices will be closed on public holidays, and major festivals can significantly affect local transportation and accommodation. It is always a good idea to check the local calendar when planning travel and activities.

Integrating into the local community

Integrating into a new community, especially in a different country, can be both an exciting and challenging process. Here are some strategies to help you integrate into the local community in the Philippines:

Language: Learning the local language, or at least some basic phrases, can be an excellent first step in integrating into the community. In the Philippines, this means learning some Filipino (Tagalog) or another local language, depending on the region where you will be living. English is widely spoken, but the effort to speak the local language will be appreciated.

Cultural Understanding: Educate yourself about Filipino culture, traditions, and etiquette. This understanding will help you navigate social situations and show respect for local customs.

Participate in Community Activities: Join local community events, celebrations, or festivals. The Philippines is known for its vibrant festivals, and participating can be a great way to get to know people and understand local traditions.

Volunteer: Volunteering can be a rewarding way to give back to the community and make connections. Look for local volunteer opportunities that align with your interests.

Join Social or Hobby Groups: Whether it is a sports team, a dance class, a cooking club, or a language exchange group, joining a group can help you meet locals who share similar interests.

Be Friendly and Open: Filipinos are known for their friendliness and hospitality. A friendly attitude and willingness to engage with people will go a long way in helping you build relationships.

Build Relationships with Neighbors: Getting to know your neighbors can make you feel more at home and connected to your community. They can also provide local insights and advice.

Support Local Businesses: Shopping at local markets, eating at local restaurants, and using local services not only supports the community economically but also provides opportunities to interact with locals.

Learn the Local Cuisine: Food is a significant part of Filipino culture. Learn about the local cuisine, try cooking Filipino dishes, and do not be afraid to try new foods.

Stay Informed: Keep up to date with local news and developments. This can help you understand the local context and issues that matter to the community.

Remember that integration takes time and patience, so do not be discouraged if it feels slow at first. Keep an open mind, be respectful, and take every opportunity to learn and engage with the community.

Practical Information

Transportation system (public and private)

The Philippines offers a variety of public and private transportation options, each providing a unique experience:

Jeepneys: The most popular and iconic form of public transport in the Philippines. Jeepneys are brightly colored, elongated jeeps that operate on fixed routes and are hailed from the roadside. Fares are generally low, but it can get crowded.

Tricycles: These are motorcycle and sidecar combinations that operate much like taxis but are typically used for shorter, local trips.

Buses: There are numerous bus services operating in cities and between towns and provinces. These include city buses, provincial buses, point-to-point (P2P) buses, and shuttle services. Some long-distance buses have air conditioning and offer more comfortable seating.

Trains: In Metro Manila, there are three elevated Light Rail Transit lines (LRT-1, LRT-2, MRT-3) and the underground Metro Manila Subway. The Philippine National Railways (PNR) also operates a commuter line in Manila and long-distance routes to the south of Luzon.

Taxis and Rideshares: Taxis are widely available in cities, and ridesharing services like Grab are prevalent, particularly in Metro Manila. Always make sure the taxi uses a meter or negotiate the fare before starting the trip.

Ferries and Bangkas: The Philippines, being an archipelago, has an extensive network of ferries and smaller bangka boats for travel between islands.

Private Vehicles: Owning a private car or motorcycle is also an option, but keep in mind that traffic can be quite heavy, especially in larger cities like Manila and Cebu. Also, the process of getting a local driver's license may require some time and paperwork.

Bicycles and Pedicabs: In some areas, particularly in less congested and more residential neighborhoods, bicycles and pedicabs (human-powered rickshaws) are used.

Flights: Domestic flights are a fast and convenient way to travel between the islands. There are several domestic airlines, including Philippine Airlines, Cebu Pacific, and AirAsia Philippines.

Each mode of transport has its advantages and considerations. Your choice would depend on factors like distance, comfort, budget, and your personal preference.

Internet and telecommunications

In the Philippines, internet and telecommunication services are widely available, especially in urban areas, but the quality and speed can vary depending on the location and service provider.

Internet:

The country has multiple Internet Service Providers (ISPs) that provide several types of connections, such as DSL, Fiber, and Satellite. The leading ISPs include PLDT, Globe Telecom, Converge, and Sky Cable. 5G is available in select areas through major telecom providers.

The average internet speed in the Philippines has improved over the years, but it may still lag some developed countries. The availability of high-speed internet also largely depends on the specific location, with urban areas and business districts typically having better service.

Many cafes, restaurants, and public areas offer free WiFi, but the connection may be unreliable. It is always best to have your own internet connection for consistent use.

Telecommunications:

The two dominant telecommunication companies providing mobile services in the Philippines are Globe Telecom and Smart Communications. They offer a wide range of services including calls, text messaging (SMS), and mobile data plans. Both prepaid and postpaid options are available.

It is easy and inexpensive to get a local SIM card. You will find vendors at the airport and in malls, convenience stores, and dedicated telecom service centers. Ensure that your phone is unlocked to accept a foreign SIM card.

Landline services are also available, often bundled with internet packages by providers like PLDT and Globe.

Internet and telecom services in the Philippines continue to evolve, and it is best to check for the most current information with the service providers or local contacts.

Safety and security tips

While the Philippines is generally a safe place to visit or live, like any other country, there are certain safety and security considerations to keep in mind:

Stay Informed about the Local Situation: Keep up-to-date with local news and be aware of any political developments, protests, or incidents that might affect safety.

Respect Local Laws and Customs: Make sure to respect local laws, religious customs, and cultural norms. This can go a long way toward ensuring your safety and well-being.

Travel with Care: Be careful when traveling, especially at night or in less populated areas. Use trusted transportation services and avoid displaying expensive possessions or flashing cash.

Secure Your Belongings: Keep your belongings always secure, particularly in crowded public places where pickpocketing can occur.

Be Aware of Scams: Be alert to potential scams, both online and in person. Common scams can involve overcharging for services, credit card fraud, or online dating scams.

Know the Emergency Numbers: In case of an emergency, you can dial 911 for immediate assistance. Also, it is a good idea to keep the contact details of your home country's embassy or consulate.

Natural Disasters: The Philippines is prone to natural disasters such as typhoons, earthquakes, and volcanic eruptions. Be aware of the local weather forecasts, sign up for any local warning systems, and familiarize yourself with evacuation plans if you are in a vulnerable area.

Health Safety: Make sure you are up to date with vaccinations, and take precautions against local health risks such as dengue fever, which is transmitted by mosquitoes. If you are unsure, consult a travel doctor before departure.

Water Safety: Tap water in the Philippines is not generally safe to drink. Stick to bottled water, and make sure food is properly cooked, especially seafood and shellfish.

Personal Safety: As in any location, be aware of your surroundings and trust your instincts. Avoid isolated areas, especially at night, and always let someone know where you are going if you are traveling alone.

Always respect local laws and customs and be sure to take the usual precautions to protect yourself and your possessions. With careful planning and caution, living in or visiting the Philippines can be a safe and enjoyable experience.

Shopping and food

The Philippines offers a diverse range of shopping and food experiences, from bustling markets to luxury malls, and from street food to high-end restaurants.

Shopping:

Malls: The Philippines is known for its large shopping malls, which are often air-conditioned and contain a wide variety of stores, restaurants, and entertainment facilities. Some of the largest and most popular malls are in Metro Manila, such as the SM Mall of Asia, SM Megamall, and Greenbelt Mall in Makati.

Markets: Traditional markets, known as "palengke," are widespread and typically sell fresh produce, meats, seafood, and locally made goods. Bargaining is common in these markets. Some famous markets include the Baguio City Market and the Dangwa Flower Market in Manila.

Night Markets: These are popular for street food, clothing, accessories, and other goods. Baguio Night Market and Sugbo Mercado in Cebu are among the notable ones.

Specialty Stores and Boutiques: For unique and high-quality items, particularly local crafts, fabrics, and designs, look for specialty stores and boutiques.

Food:

Street Food: The Philippines has a rich street food culture. Try local delicacies like balut (a fertilized duck egg), kwek-kwek (deep-fried quail eggs), isaw (grilled chicken or pig intestines), and halo-halo (a mixed dessert with fruits, jellies, beans, and crushed ice).

Local Restaurants: Local restaurants, known as "carinderias," serve home-style Filipino dishes. Lechon (roast pig), adobo (meat marinated and cooked in soy sauce, vinegar, and garlic), sinigang (sour soup), and pancit (noodles) are must-tries.

High-End Restaurants: The Philippines also offers a variety of upscale dining options, with restaurants serving both local and international cuisines.

Seafood: With its abundant coastline, the Philippines offers a wide variety of fresh seafood. Look for "dampa" markets where you can buy fresh seafood and have it cooked to order.

Fruits and Desserts: The Philippines is famous for its sweet mangoes. Other fruits like bananas, pineapples, coconuts, and durians are also common. For dessert, try bibingka (rice cake), leche flan (caramel custard), or ube (purple yam) delicacies.

Whether you are shopping or eating, you will find that the Philippines offers a mix of experiences to cater to different tastes and budgets.

Life as an Expat

Expat communities

In the Philippines, there are several active expatriate communities where newcomers can find support, friendship, and advice. Some are centered around nationalities, while others are focused on shared interests or professions. Here are a few notable ones:

American Association of the Philippines: This organization has been around for many years and offers a network for American citizens living in the Philippines. They organize social, cultural, and fundraising events.

Australian & New Zealand Social Association of the Philippines: This group is geared towards Australian and New Zealand nationals, offering a range of social and cultural activities.

The British Club Manila: This is a social club for British nationals and other English-speaking expats. They host a variety of events from casual gatherings to formal dinners.

Expats in Manila Facebook Group: This is an online community where expats share experiences, ask questions, and offer advice on living in Manila.

Internations Philippines: Internations is a global network for expats with active communities in Manila and Cebu. They organize regular events and have many sub-groups based on interests or professions.

Japanese Association Manila Inc: A community for Japanese nationals living in Manila, offering cultural events, language classes, and more.

The European Chamber of Commerce in the Philippines: While primarily a business network, the chamber also hosts networking events and provides resources that can be beneficial for European expats.

These are just a few examples, and there are many other communities out there. Some expat communities are based in specific cities, while others are countrywide. Online platforms like Facebook and Meetup can also be good places to find expat groups. It is worth checking out a few different communities to see which ones are the best fit for you.

Making local friends

Making local friends when you are an expat in a new country can be a rewarding part of the experience. Here are a few tips to help make connections with locals in the Philippines:

Learn the Language: While many Filipinos speak English, learning some Tagalog or the local dialect can go a long way in making connections. Filipinos appreciate when foreigners try to learn their language.

Join Local Clubs and Organizations: Whether it is a sports club, a hobby group, or a volunteer organization, joining local clubs can be a great way to meet locals who share your interests.

Attend Local Events and Festivals: The Philippines has many local festivals and events which are excellent opportunities to meet locals and experience the culture.

Connect Through Work or School: If you are working or studying in the Philippines, your colleagues or classmates can be a great resource for meeting new people.

Respect the Culture: Filipinos are generally warm and welcoming, but it is important to respect local customs and etiquette.

Be Open and Friendly: Filipinos are known for their friendliness and hospitality. Do not hesitate to engage in conversation or accept an invitation to a local event or family gathering.

Use social media: Many Filipinos are active on social media. Platforms like Facebook can be a good way to connect with local communities or interest groups.

Take Part in Neighborhood Activities: Depending on where you live, there may be neighborhood gatherings or community events where you can meet your neighbors.

Remember, making friends takes time, so be patient with yourself. Even small interactions can lead to meaningful connections over time.

Dealing with homesickness

Dealing with homesickness is a common challenge for many expats living abroad. Here are some tips to help manage homesickness when you are in the Philippines:

Stay Connected: Maintain regular communication with family and friends back home through video calls, emails, or social media. Sharing updates and staying connected can help you feel closer to your loved ones.

Establish a Routine: Create a routine that includes activities you enjoy or that bring you comfort. This can help create a sense of stability and familiarity in your new environment.

Explore and Engage: Immerse yourself in the local culture and explore your surroundings. Participate in local activities, festivals, or events to experience the unique aspects of the

Philippines. Engaging with the local community can help create a sense of belonging.

Find Support: Seek out expat groups, forums, or communities where you can connect with others who understand what you are going through. Sharing experiences, advice, and support with fellow expats can be helpful.

Create a Home Away from Home: Surround yourself with familiar items that remind you of home. Decorate your living space with personal mementos, photos, or familiar objects that bring you comfort.

Maintain Self-Care: Take care of your physical and mental well-being. Engage in activities that help you relax, exercise regularly, and eat a balanced diet. Engaging in self-care can boost your mood and overall well-being.

Explore Hobbies and Interests: Pursue hobbies or activities that you enjoy. Join local clubs or groups that share your interests. Engaging in activities you love can help distract you from feelings of homesickness.

Embrace the Experience: Embrace the opportunities and new experiences that come with living abroad. Keep an open mind and focus on the positive aspects of your new environment. Take advantage of the chance to learn about a new culture and grow as an individual.

If homesickness becomes overwhelming or persistent, consider seeking support from a counselor or therapist who specializes in working with expats. They can provide guidance and strategies to help you cope with homesickness and adjust to your new life in the Philippines.

Benefits and challenges specific to the Philippines

Benefits of living in the Philippines:

Warm and Hospitable Culture: Filipinos are known for their warmth, friendliness, and hospitality towards foreigners. The strong sense of community and welcoming nature can make it easier to connect with locals and feel at home.

Beautiful Natural Landscapes: The Philippines is renowned for its stunning natural landscapes, including pristine beaches, crystal-clear waters, lush mountains, and breathtaking rice terraces. Living in the Philippines gives you the opportunity to explore these natural wonders and enjoy outdoor activities.

Affordable Cost of Living: Compared to many Western countries, the cost of living in the Philippines can be relatively affordable, especially outside major cities like Manila. Housing, food, transportation, and entertainment can often be more budget friendly.

English Proficiency: English is widely spoken in the Philippines, making it easier for English-speaking expats to communicate and navigate daily life. This can facilitate smoother interactions with locals, colleagues, and service providers.

Rich Cultural Heritage: The Philippines has a diverse cultural heritage influenced by indigenous, Spanish, American, and Asian cultures. You can immerse yourself in local traditions, festivals, and historical sites, gaining a deeper appreciation for the country's unique identity.

Challenges of living in the Philippines:

Traffic and Infrastructure: Major cities in the Philippines, such as Manila, can experience heavy traffic congestion. Infrastructure in some areas may be less developed compared to other countries, leading to occasional challenges in transportation, power outages, or internet connectivity.

Weather and Natural Disasters: The Philippines is prone to typhoons, earthquakes, and volcanic activity. It is important to stay informed about weather patterns, follow safety guidelines during natural disasters, and be prepared for potential disruptions.

Bureaucracy and Red Tape: Dealing with government agencies and bureaucratic processes in the Philippines can sometimes be time-consuming and require patience. It is essential to familiarize yourself with the necessary procedures for visas, permits, and other legal requirements.

Poverty and Income Inequality: While the Philippines has made progress in recent years, poverty and income inequality remain significant challenges. Some areas may have visible disparities in living conditions and access to resources, which can be a sobering aspect of the country's social landscape.

Cultural Adjustment: Adjusting to a new culture and social norms can take time and effort. Understanding and adapting to local customs, language, and social dynamics may present initial challenges, but with an open mind and willingness to learn, these obstacles can be overcome.

As with any country, it is important to thoroughly research and understand the benefits and challenges specific to the Philippines before deciding to relocate.

Planning the Move

Timeline and checklist

Planning a move to the Philippines requires careful preparation and organization. Here is a general timeline and checklist to help you with the process:

6-12 Months Before the Move:

Research: Gather information about the Philippines, including the culture, cost of living, visa requirements, healthcare system, and local customs. Consider joining online forums or expat groups to connect with others who have experience living in the country.

Finances: Evaluate your financial situation and create a budget for the move. Consider costs such as housing, transportation, healthcare, and daily expenses. Save money for relocation expenses and any unforeseen circumstances.

Employment or Business Setup: Determine your employment options or explore business opportunities in the Philippines. Research the job market, networking opportunities, and the process for starting a business if applicable.

Visa Requirements: Understand the visa options available for your situation and determine the specific requirements for each type of visa. Contact the nearest Philippine embassy or consulate for up-to-date information.

Healthcare and Insurance: Research healthcare options and consider international health insurance coverage. Check if your current insurance policy covers you while living abroad or if you need to arrange for local coverage in the Philippines.

3-6 Months Before the Move:

Housing: Start researching housing options in your desired location in the Philippines. Consider renting or buying property based on your plans and budget. Connect with real estate agents or browse online platforms to explore available properties.

Schools and Education: If you have children, research and contact potential schools in the Philippines. Check admission requirements, curriculum, and availability of international schools if needed. Begin the enrollment process.

Packing and Shipping: Start decluttering and organizing your belongings. Decide what items to bring, sell, donate, or store. Research international shipping options if you plan to bring household items or furniture.

Notify Authorities and Services: Notify your current authorities, such as tax agencies, utilities, and banks, about your upcoming move. Arrange for the cancellation or transfer of services like internet, phone, and utilities.

1-3 Months Before the Move:

Visa Application: Begin the process of applying for the necessary visa or permits. Gather all required documents, such as passport, proof of finances, medical records, and any other supporting paperwork. Follow the guidelines provided by the Philippine embassy or consulate.

Travel Arrangements: Book your flights to the Philippines. Consider the most convenient and cost-effective options for your move.

Notify and Forward Mail: Inform your post office and relevant contacts about your change of address or arrange for mail forwarding services.

Health Check-ups and Vaccinations: Schedule a comprehensive health check-up for yourself and your family. Consult with a healthcare professional about necessary vaccinations or medications for living in the Philippines.

2-4 Weeks Before the Move:

Pack and Prepare: Start packing your belongings and labeling boxes. Make sure you have essential documents, valuables, and important items easily accessible. Prepare a separate bag with essentials for the first few days after arrival.

Notify Contacts: Inform friends, family, and important contacts about your upcoming move. Share your new contact details if available.

Cancel or Transfer Services: Cancel or transfer remaining services, such as internet, phone, and utilities, ensuring all outstanding bills are settled.

Finalize Accommodation and Transportation: Confirm your housing arrangements and transportation from the airport to your new home in the Philippines.

1 Week Before the Move:

Final Checklists: Review your checklists and ensure all necessary tasks are completed. Double-check travel arrangements, important documents, and other essentials.

Say Goodbye: Spend time with friends and family before your departure. Organize farewell gatherings or events if desired.

Currency Exchange: If needed, exchange currency to have Philippine Pesos available upon arrival.

Travel Documentation: Organize all necessary travel documents, including passports, visas, tickets, and other identification papers. Keep them easily accessible during your journey.

Moving to a new country requires thorough planning and organization. Adjust the timeline and checklist according to your specific circumstances. Do not forget to keep important documents, contact information, and essential items easily accessible during your travel to the Philippines.

What to bring

When moving to the Philippines, it is important to pack thoughtfully. Here is a list of essential items and things to consider bringing:

Travel Documents: Passports, visas, identification cards, and copies of important documents like birth certificates, marriage certificates, and medical records.

Clothing: Pack a mix of lightweight, breathable clothing suitable for the tropical climate. Include both casual attire and formal wear for special occasions. Do not forget essentials like swimwear, hats, and comfortable walking shoes.

Medications: Bring an ample supply of any prescription medications you require, along with a copy of your prescription. Some medications may not be readily available or have different brand names in the Philippines. Also, consider bringing basic over-the-counter medications for common ailments.

Toiletries and Personal Care Items: Bring your preferred toiletries, such as shampoo, conditioner, soap, toothpaste, and skincare products. While these items are available in the Philippines, you may have specific preferences.

Electronics and Appliances: Consider bringing essential electronics like laptops, smartphones, cameras, and chargers. Check if your devices are compatible with the local voltage (220V) and bring appropriate adapters or voltage converters if needed.

Important Documents: Carry important documents such as marriage certificates, academic transcripts, employment records, and insurance policies. Keep them in a secure, easily accessible folder or pouch.

Comforts of Home: Bring a few sentimental or familiar items from home that can help you feel more comfortable and remind you of home. These could be photographs, small decorative items, or favorite books.

Adapters and Power Strips: Carry power adapters suitable for the local power outlets in the Philippines. It is also helpful to have power strips to accommodate multiple devices.

Outdoor Gear: If you enjoy outdoor activities, consider bringing your own gear such as hiking boots, camping equipment, snorkeling gear, or sports equipment. These items may be more expensive or limited in selection in the Philippines.

Specialty Foods: If you have dietary restrictions or specific preferences, you may want to bring certain specialty foods or ingredients that may not be readily available in the local market.

Remember to check the airline's baggage allowance and weight restrictions to avoid excess fees. It is also important to research any customs regulations or restrictions on specific items that may apply to the Philippines.

While it is helpful to bring essential items, keep in mind that many everyday items can be purchased locally in the Philippines. Prioritize items that are not easily replaceable or may be more expensive or difficult to find in your new location.

Hiring a moving company

Hiring a moving company can greatly simplify the process of relocating to the Philippines. Here are some important factors to consider when selecting a moving company:

Research and Obtain Multiple Quotes: Research different moving companies and obtain quotes from several providers. Compare the services offered, including packing, transportation, insurance, and customs clearance.

Check Company Credentials: Ensure that the moving company is licensed and insured. Look for certifications, affiliations with international moving associations, and positive customer reviews or testimonials.

Experience and Expertise: Consider the company's experience in handling international moves, specifically to the Philippines. Ask about their knowledge of local customs regulations, import/export processes, and any specific requirements for shipping to the Philippines.

Services Provided: Determine the scope of services offered by the moving company. This may include packing, loading, transportation, customs clearance, and unpacking at your new destination. Ensure that the company can meet your specific needs and preferences.

Insurance Coverage: Inquire about the insurance coverage provided by the moving company. It is crucial to have appropriate insurance to protect your belongings during transit and in case of any damage or loss.

Cost and Payment Terms: Understand the cost structure and payment terms. Request a detailed breakdown of all costs involved, including packing materials, transportation, customs duties, and any additional fees. Clarify the payment schedule and accepted payment methods.

Timeline and Delivery: Discuss the estimated timeline for the move, including pickup, transit, and delivery to your new location in the Philippines. Seek clarification on any potential delays or factors that may affect the delivery timeframe.

Customer Support and Communication: Evaluate the company's responsiveness and communication. A reliable moving company should be prompt in addressing your inquiries, providing updates, and keeping you informed throughout the moving process.

References and Reviews: Request references from previous customers who have used the moving company's services for international moves. Additionally, check online reviews and ratings to gauge the company's reputation and customer satisfaction.

Read and Understand the Contract: Before finalizing the agreement, carefully read and understand the terms and conditions outlined in the contract. Seek clarification on any ambiguous or confusing clauses before signing.

Remember to start the process of hiring a moving company well in advance to allow time for research, obtaining quotes, and making necessary arrangements. By selecting a reputable and reliable moving company, you can have peace of mind knowing that your belongings are in capable hands during the relocation process.

Customs regulations

Understanding customs regulations is essential when moving to the Philippines to ensure a smooth and hassle-free entry of your belongings. Here are some key points to consider:

Restricted and Prohibited Items: Certain items are restricted or prohibited from being imported into the Philippines. These may include firearms, drugs, explosives, hazardous materials, certain plants and animals, counterfeit goods, and pornography. Familiarize yourself with the specific regulations to avoid any issues.

Customs Declaration: You will need to complete a customs declaration form upon arrival in the Philippines. Declare all items that you are bringing with you, including household goods, personal belongings, and any valuable or high-value items. Be accurate and thorough in your declaration.

Duty and Taxes: You may be subject to customs duties and taxes on certain items, especially if they are deemed to be of high value or in commercial quantities. The customs officials will assess the value of your belongings and apply the applicable duties and taxes accordingly. It is advisable to keep receipts or proof of purchase for valuable items.

Temporary Importation: If you are planning to bring items into the Philippines temporarily, such as for a short-term assignment or event, you may need to obtain a Temporary Importation Permit (TIP) from the Bureau of Customs. This allows you to import goods without paying customs duties and taxes, under certain conditions and for a specified period.

Customs Clearance Process: When your shipment arrives, it will go through the customs clearance process. This involves presenting the necessary documents, such as the packing list, inventory, and original passport, to the customs authorities. They will inspect the shipment and verify the contents. It is important to be present during this process or have a representative available.

Documentation and Inventory: Prepare a detailed inventory of all items you are bringing with you, including a description, quantity, and estimated value. Include this inventory with your shipment and keep a copy for your records. Provide any necessary supporting documents, such as receipts, to verify the value of high-value items.

Engaging a Licensed Customs Broker: To navigate the customs process more smoothly, it is recommended to engage a licensed customs broker. They are familiar with local regulations, documentation requirements, and customs procedures. They can assist you in preparing the necessary paperwork and guide you through the customs clearance process.

It is important to note that customs regulations and requirements can change over time. It is advisable to consult with the Philippine Bureau of Customs or a licensed customs broker for the most up-to-date information and guidance specific to your situation.

Milton Keynes UK
Ingram Content Group UK Ltd.
UKHW050523081023
430063UK00009BA/40

9 781088 079331